Praying

& Praising

through the Psalms

New King James Version

Vernet Clemons Nettles, EdD

Published by:
VCNettles Inspirations and Letters, LLC

www.vernetcnettles.com
vernetcnettles@gmail.com

Scripture from The Holy Bible, New King James Version (NKJV), Copyright 1982 Thomas Nelson.

Cover Design: Ariel Nettles

ISBN: 979-8-9913949-3-2

Printed in the United States

Table Of Contents

Introduction

As I stood in my sister-in-law's church one Sunday and sang (not quite melodiously) ***Come Thou Fount Of Every Blessing*** I was amazed and inspired. This was a song that I had not ever heard.

To me, this song beckons God to come to us. In this song, we ask God to tune our hearts and voices for praise. We ask God to teach us songs so that we can praise Him. This song is perfect. This should be our daily request, that God tunes our hearts to hear His voice. And as a result, it should be our desire to sing His praises.

As I sat through the service, my mind raced and remembered the Psalms. The Psalms – a collection of poetry, songs, praise, laments, and promise.   I remembered that I have always wanted to write something that celebrated the Psalms. This is the result of my urgency – a brief book of prayers through the Psalms.

But as there are 150 books of Psalms, there will be more of these to come.   So as always, thank you for walking and praying this journey with me.

Please enjoy this initial volume of *Praying and Praising through the Psalms*.

Come Thou Fount Of Every Blessing

Come, thou Fount of every blessing;

Tune my heart to sing Thy grace;

Streams of mercy, never ceasing,

Call for songs of loudest praise.

Teach me some melodious sonnet,

Sung by flaming tongues above;

Praise the mount! O fix me on it,

Mount of God's unchanging love!

Author: Robert Robinson
Copyright: Public Domain

Day 1

To You, O Lord, I lift up my soul.
Psalm 25:1 NKJV

Heavenly Father, thank you for all things. Father thank you for my life and my salvation. Father, thank you for all that you have given me. For all that you have given me, I desire to give back to you. Father, you have given us gifts and talents for the upbuilding of your kingdom. You have given us purpose to serve one another. Father, guide our hearts and our hands as we desire to live a life that is pleasing unto you. For these and many other blessings we pray in Jesus' name. *Amen.*

Day 2

"Show me Your ways, O Lord; Teach Your paths. Lead me in Your truth and teach me, For You are the God of my salvation; On You I wait all the day."

Psalm 25:4-5 NKJV

Heavenly Father, thank you for all things. Yes, Lord, please show us your ways and teach us your paths. Reveal to us what you would have us to do and who you would have us to be, so that we can fulfill your desires for our lives, so that our lives can be a testimony to others of your grace. Teach us, Lord, so that we may know your truth. We give ourselves to you. In Jesus' name we pray. **Amen.**

(Nettles, www.vcndailypray.com, August 26, 2016)

Day 3

"For You formed my inward parts; You covered me in my mother's womb. I will praise You, for I am fearfully and wonderfully made; Marvelous are Your works, And that my soul knows very well."

Psalm 139:13-14 NKJV

Heavenly Father, thank you for all things - for each day of life. Thank you for knowing me, even before I knew myself. Thank you for creating me - stitch by stitch. Thank you for making me so complex, so that I learn something new about me and about You, daily. Thank you, Lord, for breathing into me the breath of life. In Jesus' name we pray. *Amen.*

(Nettles, www.vcndailypray.com, August 23. 2018)

Day 4

"Your eyes saw my substance, being yet unformed. And in Your book they all were written, The days fashioned for me, When as yet there were none of them. How precious also are Your thoughts to me, O God! How great is the sum of them!"

Psalm 139:16-17 NKJV

Heavenly Father, thank you for all things - for seeing me and knowing me. Lord, you have known me since before my beginning. You saw my substance, the who I would become. You wrote my name and my life in your book. And, Lord, you think of me. Thank you, Lord. Father, help me to see myself with your eyes - wonderfully made and worthy of love. In Jesus' name we pray. *Amen.*

(Nettles, www.vcndailypray.com, May 25, 2016)

Day 5

"O LORD, You are the portion of my inheritance and my cup; You maintain my lot. The lines have fallen to me in pleasant places; Yes, I have a good inheritance."
Psalm 16:5-6 NKJV

Heavenly Father, thank you for all things.

Forgive us, Father, when we focus on what we don't have when all around us are blessings that only You have provided. Thank you, Lord, for you are our portion and our strength. Please, Lord, continue to show us your goodness and your grace, for we have a good inheritance. We are children of God. In Jesus' name we pray. *Amen.*

(Nettles, www.vcndailypray.com, March 1, 2018)

Day 6

"O God, You are my God; Early will I seek You; My soul thirsts for You; My flesh longs for You In a dry and thirsty land Where there is no water. So I have looked for You in the sanctuary, To see Your power and Your glory."

Psalm 63:1-2 NKJV

Heavenly Father, thank you for all things - for this testimony that reflects the words that fill my heart. My heart cries out for your mercy, your grace, and your comfort. My soul thirsts for you. Lord, I know that I have seen your glory. You have delivered me before. You walk with me now. You shall go before me tomorrow. Thank you, Lord for being ever-present. In Jesus' name we pray. ***Amen.***

(Nettles, www.vcndailypray.com, December 21, 2015)

Day 7

"The Lord builds up Jerusalem; He gathers together the outcasts of Israel. He heals the brokenhearted And binds up their wounds."

Psalm 147:2-3 NKJV

Heavenly Father, thank you for all things - for choosing to heal our family and bring us from exile with each other. Teach us how to forgive each other, to listen to each other, to encourage each other, to be patient with each other and to love each other. Help us, Father, to tend to each other's wounds, to give each other what is needed to aid the healing process. We depend on you, Lord, for guidance and courage to walk with each other and to walk with you. In Jesus' name we pray. *Amen*.

"The Lord is my light and my salvation; Whom shall I fear? The Lord is the strength of my life; Of whom shall I be afraid?"

Psalm 27:1 NKJV

Day 8

"I love the LORD, because He has heard My voice and my supplications. Because He has inclined His ear to me, Therefore I will call upon Him as long as I live."

Psalm 116:1-2 NKJV

Heavenly **F**ather, thank you for all things. Thank you, Lord, for being kind and merciful; for listening and hearing our prayers; and for fulfilling our every need. Father, your word reminds us that we can call on you and you will answer. Thank you for being who you are in all things. We need you and we love you. For these and many other blessings we pray and say thank you in Jesus' name. ***Amen.***

Supplications: asking earnestly or humbly

(Nettles, www.vcndailypray.com, April 20, 2016)

Day 9

"I would have lost heart, unless I had believed That I would see the goodness of the LORD In the land of the living. Wait on the LORD; Be of good courage, And He shall strengthen your heart; Wait, I say, on the LORD!"

Psalm 27:13-14 NKJV

Heavenly Father, thank you for all things.

Thank you, Lord, for your Word that reminds me that trials are a part of life - but if we believe, trust, and have faith in You, there is goodness to come - not just in heaven, but here on earth. GLORY!!! Thank you, Lord. Help me; teach me to wait on your promises, on your resolutions, and on your will for my life. And while I wait, Father, guide me in service to you and for others. In Jesus' name we pray. *Amen*

(Nettles, www.vcndailypray.com, July 12, 2017)

Day 10

"And those who know Your name will put their trust in You; For You, LORD, have not forsaken those who seek You."

Psalm 9:10 NKJV

Heavenly Father, thank you for all things - for the journey. With each step you prove your love and faithfulness toward each of us. We love you and we are grateful for your ever presence. With each step, we learn more and more to trust you. We seek you, Lord - to hear your voice and follow your way – for the righteous shall not be forsaken. Thank you, Lord. In Jesus' name we pray. *Amen.*

Righteous – doing with is right in God's sight; living in right relationship with God and all creation

(Nettles, www.vcndailypray.com, December 9. 2015)

Day 11

"Search me, O God, and know my heart; Try me, and know my anxieties; And see if there is any wicked way in me, And lead me in the way everlasting."

Psalm 139:23-24 NKJV

Heavenly Father, thank you for all things.

Lord, search my heart; show me the places within me that are not pleasing to you. Show me the places of my unresolved sin, my unresolved personal shortcomings, so that I may know and seek your forgiveness and guidance. Lead me, Lord, as I desire to grow closer to you. In Jesus' name we pray. *Amen.*

(Nettles, www.vcndailypray.com, April 4, 2016)

Day 12

"The LORD will perfect that which concerns me; Your mercy, O LORD, endures forever; Do not forsake the works of Your hands."
Psalm 138:8 NKJV

Heavenly Father, thank you for all things - for your perfect peace. Thank you, Father, for reminding me that you will work out all things that concern me. Help me to stop trying to work things out according to my will. Guide me to lean into your plans for me. Thank you for your faithfulness that comforts me, and your mercy that endures forever. In Jesus' name we pray and rest. **Amen.**

(Nettles, www.vcndailypray.com, February 17, 2017)

Day 13

"Unless the LORD builds the house, They labor in vain who build it; Unless the LORD guards the city, The watchman stays awake in vain."

Psalm 127:1 NKJV

Heavenly **F**ather, thank you for all things. Thank you for reminding us to put you first in all things - relationships, family, work, health, _____ - otherwise our work is useless. Lord, we labor unnecessarily over many things before we talk to you. Show us, Lord, your way, your will, and your plan for our lives. Build our lives, our homes, our _____. Keep our surroundings, so that when we watch and pray, we are secure in you. In Jesus' name we pray. *Amen.*

(Nettles, www.vcndailypray.com, May 26, 2016)

Day 14

"Oh, give thanks to the Lord! Call upon His name; Make known His deeds among the peoples!　Remember His marvelous works which He has done, His wonders, and the judgments of His mouth,"

Psalm 105:1, 5 NKJV

Heavenly Father, thank you for all things. We give you honor and praise for all that you have done and all that you will do. We thank you for your blessings and deliverance in the chapters of our lives, and we wait in glorious expectation of blessings to come. We thank you for the miracles of healing, _____, _____, and _____. We look to you for strength, and we seek your face - for you alone are God. In Jesus' name we pray. *Amen.*

(Nettles, www.vcndailypray.com, January 1, 2015)

"My flesh and my heart fail; But God is the strength of my heart and my portion forever."

Psalm 73:26 NKJV

Day 15

"When the LORD brought back the captivity of Zion, We were like those who dream. Then our mouth was filled with laughter, And our tongue with singing. Then they said among the nations, "The LORD has done great things for them." The LORD has done great things for us, And we are glad."
Psalm 126:1-3 NKJV

Heavenly Father, thank you for all things – for the gifts of restoration, laughter, and joy. Father, restoration reminds us that our struggle is temporary. Thank you for your joy which spills over into laughter, so that others can see and know your grace. We are grateful for every opportunity to laugh and sing because it reminds us of your love. For these thy gifts, we thank you. In Jesus' name we pray. *Amen.*

(Nettles, www.vcndailypray.com, February 2, 2017)

Day 16

"It is good to give thanks to the LORD, And to sing praises to Your name, O Most High; To declare Your lovingkindness in the morning, And Your faithfulness every night,"

Psalm 92:1-2 NKJV

Heavenly Father, thank you for all things - for the opportunity to say Thank You. Father. I thank you for _____, _____, and _____. Your kindness and faithfulness are in our every breath and in our every circumstance, regardless of how they may first appear. Today we simply sing and shout your praise. In Jesus' name we pray. *Amen.*

(Nettles, www.vcndailypray.com, February 17, 2017)

Day 17

"And let the beauty of the LORD our God be upon us, And establish the work of our hands for us; Yes, establish the work of our hands."

Psalm 90:17 NKJV

Heavenly Father, thank you for all things - for the work you have charged me (us) to do. I (We) pray that your favor rests upon me (us), and that you establish the work of my (our) hands. Bless the work and the worker, so that in its success all the glory is to you. Guide me (us), Lord. In Jesus' name we pray. *Amen.*

(Nettles, www.vcndailypray.com, April 15, 2016)

Day 18

"Blessed be the Lord, Because He has heard the voice of my supplications! The Lord is my strength and my shield; My heart trusted in Him, and I am helped; Therefore my heart greatly rejoices, And with my song I will praise Him."

Psalm 28:6-7 NKJV

Heavenly Father, thank you for all things. Thank you, Lord, for hearing my cries - to hear your voice, and begin anew with you. Thank you for being my strength and my shield. There have been trials and triumphs, and I am grateful that you have allowed me to see victory. My heart rejoices as I look forward to new adventures with you. Thank you, Lord, for your gifts; guide me to use them in praise and service to you. In Jesus' name we pray. *Amen*.

(Nettles, www.vcndailypray.com, January 24, 2025)

27

Day 19

"One thing I have desired of the LORD, That will I seek: That I may dwell in the house of the LORD All the days of my life, To behold the beauty of the LORD, And to inquire in His temple. For in the time of trouble He shall hide me in His pavilion; In the secret place of His tabernacle He shall hide me; He shall set me high upon a rock."

Psalm 27:4-5 NKJV

Heavenly Father, thank you for all things - for your everlasting Love. Thank you for every opportunity to dwell in your Spirit when I study your Word, for the joy of knowing that You are ever-present, and for the security in knowing that you are my protection. Thank you for reminding us to desire to seek you, and you will dwell in our hearts, comfort us, and hide us in your Love. In Jesus' name we pray. *Amen.*

(Nettles, www.vcndailypray.com, August 24, 2018)

Day 20

"Oh, sing to the Lord a new song! Sing to the Lord, all the earth. Sing to the Lord, bless His name; Proclaim the good news of His salvation from day to day. Declare His glory among the nations, His wonders among all peoples. For the Lord is great and greatly to be praised; He is to be feared above all gods."

Psalm 96:1-4 NKJV

Heavenly **F**ather, thank you for all things.

Father, this day, we sing a song of Thanksgiving. Father, we bless your name and shout Glory Hallelujah, for you are great and greatly to be praised. As we walk hand in hand with you - we ask for your grace and mercy, your purpose for our lives and your guiding hand. We dedicate ourselves to you as we look forward to these thy gifts. In Jesus' name we pray. ***Amen.***

(Nettles, www.vcndailypray.com, January 1, 2017)

"I will praise You, O Lord, with my whole heart; I will tell of all Your marvelous works. I will be glad and rejoice in You; I will sing praise to Your name, O Most High."

Psalm 9:1-2 NKJV

Day 21

"Bless the Lord, O my soul; And all that is within me, bless His holy name! Bless the Lord, O my soul, And forget not all His benefits: Who forgives all your iniquities, Who heals all your diseases, Who redeems your life from destruction, Who crowns you with lovingkindness and tender mercies, Who satisfies your mouth with good things, So that your youth is renewed like the eagle's."

Psalm 103:1-5 NKJV

Heavenly **F**ather, thank you for all things. We praise your name today and always. Thank you for the forgiveness of our sins, for the healing of our illnesses-physical, spiritual, and emotional. Thank you for the construction and reconstruction of our lives when we are turning things upside down and inside out.   Thank you for your loving kindness and your tender mercies that are new every morning.   Father, thank you for being our everything! In Jesus' name we pray, praise, and celebrate your goodness. *Amen.*

Benediction

The Lord shall preserve you from all evil;
He shall preserve your soul. The Lord shall
preserve your going out and your coming
in From this time forth, and even
forevermore.

Psalm 121:7 – 8 NKJV

"God be merciful to us and bless us, And
cause His face to shine upon us,

Selah"

Psalm 67:1 NKJV

Prayers / Blessings / Praises

Prayers / Blessings / Praises

_____

_____

_____

_____

_____

_____

_____

_____

_____

_____

_____

_____

_____

_____

_____

Prayers / Blessings / Praises

_____

_____

_____

_____

_____

_____

_____

_____

_____

_____

_____

_____

_____

_____

_____

_____

_____

Prayers / Blessings / Praises

_____

_____

_____

_____

_____

_____

_____

_____

_____

_____

_____

_____

_____

_____

Additional Author's Works

Why Should I Be Bound?   Musings on a Journey with God (2018)

Pray, Praise and Be Encouraged - A 21-day devotional (2020)

Prayers for a Friend (2021)

Moments of Grace: A New Beginning (2023)

Walking With Gace: A Fresh Start (2023)

Sufficient Grace: New Mercies Each Day (2023)

Prayers for the Journey (2023)

Prayers for your Fasting Journey (2024)

To purchase visit:

www.vernetcnettles.com

www.amazon.com

About the Author

Vernet Clemons Nettles, EdD is a parent, retired educator, speaker and writing coach. Throughout the years, she has served in various capacities of church service education administration.

Dr. Nettles enjoys seeking Christ, researching the Word of God, and relishing in the aha moments of God's promises.

Let's stay connected:

www.vernetcnettles.com

vernetcnettles@gmail.com

www.ingramcontent.com/pod-product-compliance
Lightning Source LLC
Chambersburg PA
CBHW070036110426
42741CB00035B/2789